FOR JOSH

Editor: Elizabeth Mann
Design: Lesley Ehlers Design

Copyright © 2003 Mikaya Press
Illustrations Copyright © Tom McNeely

Library of Congress Cataloging-in Publication Data

Waldman, Stuart, 1941–
   We asked for nothing : the remarkable journey of Cabeza de Vaca/ by Stuart Waldman;
illustrated by Tom McNeely.
      p. cm.–(A great explorers book)
   Summary: An Account of the travels of the Spanish explorer Cabeza de Vaca through Texas
and Mexico from 1528 through 1536, looking particularly at his relations with the native
people with whom he shared his journeys.
   Includes bibliographical references and index.
   ISBN 1-931414-07-6
   1. Núñez Cabeza de Vaca, Alvar, 16th cent.—Juvenile literature. 2. America—Discovery
and exploration—Spanish—Juvenile literature. 3. America–Description and travel—Juvenile
literature. 4. Indians, Treatment of—History—16th century—Juvenile literature. 5. Indians
of North America—History—16th century—Juvenile literature. 6.
Explorers—America—Biography—Juvenile literature. 7.
Explorers—Spain—biography—Juvenile literature. [Cabeza de Vaca, Alvar Núñez, 16th
cent. 2. Explorers. 3. America—Discovery and exploration—Spanish. 4.
Indians—Treatment. 5. Indians of North America—History—16th century.] I.
McNeely,
   Tom, ill II. Title. III. Series.

E125.N9W35 2003
970.01'6'092--dc21

                                        2003046472

Printed in China

We Asked For Nothir

The Remarkable Journey of Cabeza de Vaca